I0164960

# The Superiority of Christ

## A study in the epistle to the Hebrews

## W M Henry

**ISBN: 978-1-78364-451-3**

**The Open Bible Trust,**
**Fordland Mount, Upper Basildon,**
**Reading, RG8 8LU, UK.**

**www.obt.org.uk**

Unless indicated otherwise Scripture quotations are taken from the Holy Bible, New International Version Anglicised Copyright © 1979, 1984, 2011 Biblica. Used by permission of Hodder & Stoughton Ltd, an Hachette UK company. All rights reserved. 'NIV' is a registered trademark of Biblica UK trademark number 1448790.

# The Superiority of Christ

## Contents

**Page**

# Introduction

# Introduction

The epistle to the Hebrews is one of the longest epistles in the New Testament, with only Romans and 1 Corinthians containing more chapters. Although the writer is not identified in the letter, the intended readership is clear. The entire book is steeped in the religious concepts and history of Israel and is clearly written with a Jewish audience in mind.

The purpose of the epistle is also clear; the major part of the epistle shows the superiority of the Lord Jesus Christ to the religious system established by Moses in the Old Testament. This is startling in its implications, because Israel's system of worship, and all the rites and rituals that went along with it, were developed not as Moses' ideas, but on the basis of God's revelation to him. What the epistle to the Hebrews reveals is that all of these have been superseded by the Lord Jesus Christ. Not only so, but the Levitical priesthood, the Law and the old covenant, although instituted on God's instructions, were intended to be temporary. They were pointing towards the One who was to come, who would open up the way back to God for fallen man.

One of the key words in the epistle is the Greek word *kreitton*, usually translated "better". This word occurs 13 times in Hebrews, compared with only six times in the rest of the New Testament and the epistle aims to show how much the new covenant, established by the Lord Jesus, is "better" than what went before.

The book also puts emphasis on the word *teleioo* (or related words) meaning "perfect" in the sense of "complete" or "mature" or "completely fit for purpose," rather than meaning morally perfect. For example, in Hebrews 7:19 we read:

> ... (for the law made nothing *perfect*) and a *better* hope is introduced, by which we draw near to God.

The Lord Jesus became *perfect* through suffering (Hebrews 2:10), He entered into a more *perfect* tabernacle (Hebrews 9:11) and by His sacrifice, He made those who are being made holy, *perfect forever* (Hebrews 10:14).

The major section from the opening chapter of Hebrews to 10:18 systematically examines key features of the Jewish religious system and shows, with arguments supported from Old Testament texts, that the Lord Jesus is superior to all of them. The Lord Jesus is shown as being superior to the prophets, to angels, to Moses himself and to Joshua. His priesthood is shown as being better than the Levitical priesthood, established through Aaron, and the new covenant He established supersedes the old covenant administered through the Law by the Levitical priests. Finally, in a glorious climax, we discover that His sacrifice on the cross achieved what all the sacrifices of bulls and goats could never achieve – real cleansing from moral guilt, and an opening up of the way back to God.

This book considers each of the aspects of the Jewish religious system identified by the writer of Hebrews and explores his arguments demonstrating the superiority of Christ at each stage. Many of the arguments are not easy to follow, as we are not Jews, steeped in the Mosaic Law, with its rites, rituals and rules. Also, the author sometimes doubles back on himself to repeat points for emphasis, or introduces ideas that he is going to develop more fully in later chapters. In a booklet of this size it is impossible to discuss all the arguments exhaustively. However, I hope that, by considering these passages in Hebrews, we may have a better insight into the perfection of God's plan for His people. How He worked all His purposes out for them and how He will bring His purposes to fruition on the day when both houses of Israel will be fully restored with His law in their minds and hearts (Jeremiah 31:33).

# The Son's superiority to the prophets

# The Son's superiority to the prophets Hebrews 1:1-3

The epistle to the Hebrews starts very abruptly. Unlike all the other epistles in the New Testament, with the exception of John's letters, there is no reference to the author. There is also no mention of his intended readership, although the title and theme of the book and the reference to "our forefathers" in the opening verse, would suggest that he is a Jew writing for Jews. Any Gentile readers would have been in the dark as to the features of Israel's worship and history, so most of the epistle would have been lost on them.

## God's revelation in the form of Son (Hebrews 1:1-2)

The first three verses of chapter 1 set out the superiority of God's revelation of Himself in the Son, over and against His earlier revelation through the prophets. Over a long period of time God had, in different ways, spoken through the prophets but now "in these last days he has spoken to us by his Son" (Hebrews 1:2). The contrast is between the limited, human revelation through the mouths of the prophets and the physical presence of the all-powerful, pre-existent One – who was with God and who was God (John 1:1). God had appeared in person.

The timing of the revelation was also critical. Hebrews 1:2 says that it was "in these last days," which we might think of as no more significant than "recently." However, the Greek suggests a break between the era of the prophets and the era brought in by the Lord. The RSV translates the phrase "at the end of these days." The coming of the Lord Jesus Christ meant that life on earth would never be the same again.

The prophets only had a partial vision. Their view was unclear and clouded by local events. Many prophets spoke into a local situation and their outlook was largely bounded by the confines of their own lives and contemporary culture. Although they understood that they were speaking of things beyond their own time and location, they did not have a full picture of what they were describing. As the Lord Jesus told His disciples:

> "Many prophets and kings wanted to see what you see but did not see it and to hear what you hear but did not hear it." (Luke 10:24)

Peter describes the prophets' meticulous work:

> Concerning this salvation, the prophets, who spoke of the grace that was to come to you, searched intently and with the greatest care, trying to find out the time and circumstances to which the Spirit of Christ in them was pointing when he predicted the sufferings of Christ and the glories that would follow. It was revealed to them that they were not serving themselves but you, when they spoke of the things that have now been told you by those who have preached the gospel to you by the Holy Spirit sent from heaven. Even angels long to look into these things. (1 Peter 1:10-12)

Both the Old Testament prophets and those preaching the gospel to Peter's readers spoke by the power of the Holy Spirit. The words of the prophets were not errors that had to be corrected later. But the clarity of their revelation of God's plans and purposes cannot be compared with the authenticity of this final revelation of the Son in person. Those who lived in the new age introduced by the presence of the Son were immensely privileged – prophets, kings and even angels had wanted to investigate these things but had not been able to do so.

## The characteristics of the Son (Hebrews 1:2-3)

Having declared the superiority of the form of this new revelation, Hebrews 1:2-3 sets before us the characteristics of the One being revealed. And what a magnificent statement of the glories of the Lord Jesus Christ it is! These brief sentences echo other Scriptures and give us a wonderful summary of His greatness.

*... whom he appointed heir of all things (Hebrews 1:2)*

The Son is supreme. Colossians 1 reveals the Lord Jesus as the "firstborn" (i.e. heir) in 2 dimensions. First, in verse 15, He is the firstborn over the original creation and then in verse 18, He is firstborn from among the dead. This, according to verse 18 was:
> so that in everything he might have the supremacy.

As Colossians 1:16 says,

> By him all things were created: things in heaven and on earth, visible and invisible, whether thrones or powers or rulers or authorities; all things were created by him and for him.

Part of the reason why He is the heir is because He was also the creator.

*... through whom he made the universe (Hebrews 1:2)*

The Son was the creating power of the Godhead. John 1:3 spells out His role in creation:

> Through him all things were made; without him nothing was made that has been made.

He is the heir and He was the creator of all. In fact He is God Himself.

*The Son is the radiance of God's glory and the exact representation of his being (Hebrews 1:3)*

The Lord Jesus is not the greatest of God's creations because He is not a created being. He is, in the words of the Christmas carol, "begotten not created," a theme which is developed further in Hebrews 1. He is "in very nature God" (Philippians 2:6). He is "the image of the invisible God" (Colossians 1:15).

In the second chapter of the same epistle Paul goes on to state that:

> ... in Christ all the fullness of the Deity lives in bodily form (Colossians 2:9)

It is important to see that Paul in this passage expresses this truth in the present tense. He is not referring merely to Christ's earthly body. Now, in His risen, ascended, glorified form, He still has the fullness of Deity in bodily form.

If we want to see what God is like, we must look to Jesus. The wonderful truth is not just that Jesus is like God, but that God is like Jesus.

*... sustaining all things by his powerful word (Hebrews 1:3)*

Here the writer picks up on the ongoing work of Christ. He is the means by which divine providence operates. This phrase may conjure up pictures in our minds of the Lord Jesus holding the planets in their orbits, or enabling the sun to continue sending out its energy, but the writer means more than this. There is a suggestion that the whole of creation is moving in a controlled way towards a predetermined destiny or climax. Paul sums up this over-riding purpose when he speaks of the mystery of God's will:

> ... to be put into effect when the times will have reached their fulfilment – to bring all things together under one head, even Christ. (Ephesians 1:10)

These opening verses of Hebrews are breathtaking. The Lord Jesus is presented as the creator of all, the owner of all, and the One who holds everything together. He is, in fact, the exact representation of God, revealed to mankind in a way that far supersedes the earlier, partial revelation of God through the mouths of the prophets.

But there is still more. He is also the means by which God's purposes of redemption were accomplished.

*After he had provided purification for sins, he sat down at the right hand of the Majesty in heaven (Hebrews 1:3)*

The Lord Jesus did not come to earth merely to reveal His Father; He came to die as a sacrifice for sins. By doing so He accomplished something no prophet, or indeed no man, could ever achieve – an effective means by which we could be made truly clean, not in the symbolic sense of the Old Testament animal sacrifices, but in reality. Hebrews 10 explores the superiority of His sacrifice in more depth but, at present, the writer notes the point briefly and moves on.

Hebrews 1:3 finishes with the Lord seated at the right hand of God in heaven. Again, the implications of this are explored later in the epistle – in chapters 8 and 10. The action of sitting down suggests the completion of the work He was sent to do. We have an effective sacrifice; there is a sure and certain hope; we have encountered God Himself.

God's revelation of Himself in Christ was a much clearer and fuller revelation than that given through the Old Testament prophets. That earlier revelation was incomplete and limited but with the coming of Christ the focus is much sharper. As the Lord Himself said:

Anyone who has seen me has seen the Father. (John 14:9)

# The Son's superiority to angels

# The Son's superiority to angels Hebrews 1:4-2:9

Throughout the Old Testament we frequently read of angels playing an important part in God's interaction with the nation of Israel. For example, angels rescued Lot from Sodom (Genesis 19:15-17), prevented Abraham from sacrificing Isaac (Genesis 22:11) and stopped Balaam from speaking against Israel (Numbers 22:35). Angels also encouraged Gideon (Judges 6:12), came to predict the birth of Samson (Judges 13:3-5), and provided food for Elijah when he was on the run from Jezebel (1 Kings 19:5). God had used angels extensively in working out His purposes and in communicating with His people. The writer to the Hebrews now turns to show that the Lord Jesus is superior to these powerful beings.

He does this initially by affirming the Son's superiority in verse 4 before quoting seven Old Testament Scriptures which demonstrate that superiority.

> So he became as much superior to the angels as the name he has inherited is superior to theirs. (Hebrews 1:4)

## Seven Old Testament References
## (Hebrews 1:5-14)

1. *Verse 5a – Psalm 2*
   For to which of the angels did God ever say, "You are my Son; today I have become your Father."?

Psalm 2 is a Messianic Psalm. The immediate context is the coronation of one of Israel's kings (possibly Solomon) but the meaning of the Psalm extends far beyond its local setting. Psalm 2:8-9 speaks of this King ruling the earth with an iron sceptre. In the New Testament the psalm is applied to Christ in Acts 13:33. The position of ruling the nations is offered by the Lord Jesus to His overcoming servants:

> To him who overcomes and does my will to the end, I will give authority over the nations – He will rule them with an iron sceptre; he will dash them to pieces like pottery – just as I have received authority from my Father. (Revelation 2:26-27)

No angel could claim such a position. Although Job 1:6 (margin) refers to angels as a group as "sons of God" no one angel is given that title anywhere in Scripture. It is reserved for the Lord Jesus.

2. *Verse 5b – 2 Samuel 7:14*
   "I will be his Father, and he will be my Son"

Again the local context of this verse is Solomon, who was given the task of building the temple. But there is a suggestion that the Lord, in speaking to David about Solomon, was looking beyond him to David's greater Son, whose kingdom would last forever. As the Lord says in 2 Samuel 7:16:

Your house and your kingdom will endure forever before
me; your throne will be established forever.

No angel was ever given such a privilege. Both these references
in Hebrews 1:5 not only show the Lord Jesus as Son of the Father
but also (in the setting of His place as King of Israel), as Son of
David – a unique position.

3. *Verse 6 – Deuteronomy 32:43*
   And again, when God brings his firstborn into the world,
   he says, "Let all God's angels worship him."

In the Greek translation of the Old Testament (Septuagint) the
hymn of Moses in Deuteronomy 32:43 includes the instruction for
the angels to worship the Son. Scripture is clear that only God is
worthy of worship. Satan tried to persuade the Lord Jesus to
worship him in return for a quick path to glory but the Lord was
adamant:

"Worship the Lord your God and serve Him only."
(Matthew 4:10)

In Revelation 19 John, overwhelmed by what he was seeing,
turned to worship the angel who revealed these things to him.

At this I fell at his feet to worship him. But he said to me,
"Do not do it! I am a fellow servant with you and with
your brothers who hold to the testimony of Jesus. Worship
God!" (Revelation 19:10)

Angels, far from being objects of worship, are fellow servants
with us and God's will is that they, like we, should worship the
Son.

*4. Verse 7 – Psalm 104:4*

In speaking of the angels he says, "He makes his angels winds, his servants flames of fire."

Angels are depicted in Psalm 104 (see Authorised Version) as God's servants, in the metaphors of winds and flames of fire. They are messengers of God rather than God Himself. By contrast, the Son reigns in His own right, as verse 8 explains.

*5. Verses 8-9 – Psalm 45:6-7*

But about the Son he says, "Your throne O God, will last for ever and ever, and righteousness will be the sceptre of your kingdom. You have loved righteousness and hated wickedness; therefore God, your God, has set you above your companions by anointing you with the oil of joy."

Again in these verses the Son is seen as king and is addressed, interestingly, in the Psalm as God. As in verse 5 He is seen as the ruler over an everlasting kingdom – a kingdom characterised by truth, humility and righteousness (Psalm 45:4), and by justice (Psalm 45:6). This is a vision of the Messianic kingdom upon the earth, which the Lord will set up when He returns.

*6. Verses 10-12 – Psalm 102:25-27*

He also says, "In the beginning, O Lord, you laid the foundations of the earth, and the heavens are the work of your hands. They will perish, but you remain; they will wear out like a garment. You will roll them up like a robe; like a garment they will be changed. But you remain the same, and your years will never end."

The imagery in this Psalm shows the Lord in the beginning at the heart of creation and also, at the end, as the One who will roll up the universe like a robe. We have already seen in Hebrews 1:2

that it was through Christ that the universe was made. We now find that it is He who will bring this present creation to a close. He is Sovereign over all creation – the unchanging Lord (see also Hebrews 13:8). No angel can make such a claim.

7.  *Verses 13-14 – Psalm 110:1*
To which of the angels did God ever say, "Sit at my right hand until I make your enemies a footstool for your feet"? Are not all angels ministering spirits sent to serve those who will inherit salvation?

These verses are the pinnacle of the Son's superiority. In this Psalm David is speaking about the risen glorified Lord Jesus, as Peter confirms in his sermon in Acts 2:34-36. The invitation to sit at the right hand of the Father was never offered to angels for it belongs to the Son as a matter of right. Paul also reveals the Lord Jesus:

> ... seated ... at his (the Father's) right hand in the heavenly realms, far above all rule and authority, power and dominion, and every title that can be given, not only in the present age but also in the one to come. And God placed all things under his feet and appointed him to be head over everything for the church, which is his body, the fullness of him who fills everything in every way. (Ephesians 1:20-23)

A position like this was never offered to any angel. The Son is supreme.

So what is the function of angels in relation to the ministry and work of the Lord Jesus? Hebrews 1 concludes with the statement that they are ...

... ministering spirits sent to serve those who will inherit salvation. (Hebrews 1:14)

It is interesting to notice the ministering work of angels in relation to the Lord Jesus during His earthly life. When He was exhausted, after forty days of temptation in the wilderness, we read that angels came and attended Him (Matthew 4:11). In Gethsemane, as He was burdened down by the thought of what lay before Him, an angel came and strengthened Him (Luke 22:43). On resurrection morning, it was an angel who rolled away the stone from the cave (Matthew 28:2). The angels played a supporting, enabling role, but it was the Lord Jesus who withstood the temptations, who steadfastly went to the cross and who rose triumphantly from the dead. Although angels have an important supporting function to carry out, they could not redeem mankind. It took the work of the glorious Lord Jesus to do this.

## A little lower than the angels? (Hebrews 2:5-9)

The ministry of angels, then, was to serve and Hebrews 2 opens with a warning that if the message brought by these angels in Old Testament times was binding, how much more important was it to heed the message brought through the superior revelation of Christ? For God's purpose was that "the world to come" (Hebrews 2:6) was to be subject not to angels but to mankind. The writer quotes Psalm 8 in Hebrews 2:6-8 – a Psalm marvelling that the God of Creation should care for insignificant humans. Yet this is the case and though He has made us a little lower than angels, our destiny is to be crowned with glory and honour and with everything under our feet.

However, as with the other Messianic Psalms, there is a deeper meaning than what is apparent on the surface. Reference to the "son of man" in Psalm 8 could just be an idiomatic way of saying "the man in the street" but from Daniel 7 and the teaching of Jesus (e.g. John 6:53), it is clear that this phrase is used of the Messiah. The problem is, as Hebrews 2:8 points out, we do not at present see all the earth under the feet of mankind – at least, not in the context of the responsible stewardship envisaged in Genesis 1. Adam sinned and his descendants have abused the world and the creatures living in it. Creation is crying out for deliverance (Romans 8:20-22). And that deliverance will come through the work of the second Adam, the Lord Jesus Christ.

Mankind may have failed but Hebrews 2:9 opens with the triumphant cry "But we see Jesus ..." He, as Son of Man and representative of mankind, was made a little lower than the angels. At present, we do not see everything subject to Him on earth, but, because He tasted death for us, He has been crowned with honour and glory, and has been restored to His rightful place of glory at the right hand of God. The ideas in Hebrews 2 are echoed in Philippians 2 – the great chapter that describes the Lord's voluntary humiliation of Himself, not just to be lower than angels but to go to death on a cross. But He is no longer lower than angels. Instead, because of His obedience to death:

> God exalted him to the highest place and gave him the name that is above every name, that at the name of Jesus every knee should bow, in heaven and on earth and under the earth, and every tongue confess that Jesus Christ is Lord, to the glory of God the Father. (Philippians 2:9-11)

# The Son's superiority to Moses

# The Son's superiority to Moses
# Hebrews 3:1-19

## Faithful as a son (Hebrews 3:1-6)

Chapter 3 opens with the word "therefore," which takes us back to what was said before. Because of Christ's superiority to prophets and angels, and because of what He has accomplished, these Hebrew believers are to fix their thoughts on Him – their apostle and high priest. The word "apostle" means "one who is sent" and the first one who was sent was Moses, who released the Israelites from bondage. The first great priest was Aaron. The writer is going to discuss the Lord Jesus in relation to the Aaronic priesthood in chapter 5 but for now he focuses on a comparison between Jesus and Moses.

Writing to Hebrew Christians, the author needs to be very careful. At that time there were "thousands of Jews (who) have believed, and all of them are zealous for the law" (Acts 21:20). Moses was revered by this group of Christians and there was a danger that the writer of the epistle could cause serious offence to his readers. He begins in verse 2 by offering a straight comparison between Jesus and Moses – both were faithful. In Numbers 12:7 the Lord declares Moses to be "faithful in all my house" and Jesus, here in Hebrews 3:2, is stated to be faithful to the One who appointed Him.

It is hard to know what is meant by "all my house" in this context. It could refer to the nation of Israel but some writers understand it as a reference to the Tabernacle, which is described as the house of God several times in the Old Testament, and to its successor, the Temple. It was Moses who received instruction from the Lord on the building of the Tabernacle. However, the house that the Lord Jesus is building is not a physical construction, but the people of God (see Hebrews 3:6).

*The house and the builder*

From verse 3, the writer begins to emphasise the differences between Moses and Jesus. Moses was faithful and is someone to be honoured. But Jesus was worthy of greater honour than Moses because He was the builder of the house. Moses, by contrast was only a member (albeit a very important one) of the house.

It is interesting that the writer here slips easily between attributing this building work to God and to the Lord Jesus. In verse 3 it is Jesus who is the builder. In verse 4 we read that God builds everything. We have already seen this truth in the context of creation. In the beginning God created, but Hebrews 1:2 tells us that it was through the Lord Jesus that the universe was made. Here too, the "house" is God's, but it is Jesus who is the builder.

When Simon Peter confessed the Lord Jesus as the Christ, the Son of the living God, Jesus replied,

> I tell you that you are Peter and on this rock (i.e. Peter's confession) *I will build my church*. (Matthew 16:18)

*The servant and the son*

In verses 5 and 6, the writer shows a further contrast between Moses and the Lord. Moses was faithful as a servant (verse 5), whereas Christ is faithful as a son over God's house (verse 6). Moses, as a faithful servant, led the Israelites out of Egypt and into the desert, mediating between them and the Lord, through all their grumblings and rebellion. Frequently he pleaded with the Lord not to destroy them for their failures. But the Lord Jesus was at a different level altogether. He is the builder of God's house and, unlike Moses, great though he was, Jesus is Son and Heir. As Wright observes:

> Moses matters but Jesus matters even more; Moses was a true servant of God but Jesus is God's son. You don't diminish Moses by making Jesus superior to him; you give him his rightful place, which is a place of honour even though it's not the supreme honour. (T Wright, *Hebrews for Everyone*, p23)

In verse 6, for the first time in this letter, we find Jesus described by the title "Christ." It is surprising that it is not until chapter 3 of a book written to Hebrews that Jesus is given the title of Messiah – the fulfiller of Jewish expectation. He is the One to whom Moses and all the Law were pointing.

Verse 6 declares that it is believers who are God's "house" but gives the first intimation of a warning that to remain as members of that house, the readers need to hold on to their courage and the hope of which they boast. The remainder of the chapter contains an important lesson for these new Jewish Christians, drawn from the history of their own nation.

## A warning lesson from the Old Testament
## (Hebrews 3:7-19)

Moses, though inferior to Christ, was a great servant of God and the author of Hebrews sees a danger that the Jewish believers who are following the Lord Jesus could fall into the same trap that snared the Jewish nation who followed Moses into the wilderness. That generation failed to heed the evidence of God's guiding presence with them and to trust Him and this had brought God's displeasure on them. How much more serious would it be for those who had seen God in action in Christ's earthly ministry, and in the work of the apostles during the Acts period if they turned away from Him. As Hebrews 10:28-29 explains:

> Anyone who rejected the law of Moses died without mercy on the testimony of two or three witnesses. How much more severely do you think a man deserves to be punished who has trampled the Son of God under foot, who has treated as an unholy thing the blood of the covenant that sanctified him, and who has insulted the Spirit of grace?

In fact, in Hebrews 6:4-6, the author goes as far as to say:

> It is impossible for those who have once been enlightened, who have tasted the heavenly gift, who have shared in the Holy Spirit, who have tasted the goodness of the word of God and the powers of the coming age, if they fall away, to be brought back to repentance, because to their loss they are crucifying the Son of God all over again and subjecting him to public disgrace.

These, then, are serious issues. It is worth tracing out the writer's arguments.

## The Israelites' refusal to trust

Hebrews 3:7-11 opens with a quotation from Psalm 95. This Psalm starts with an invitation to the Lord's people to come together to praise Him for His greatness and His mighty acts but it then moves into a warning not to be like their ancestors, who rebelled against Moses and refused to obey the Lord. The Psalm highlights the incidents at Meribah and Massah, which are outlined in Exodus 17:1-7. There Moses struck the rock to produce water for the thirsty people and their animals. The Israelites, however, repeatedly refused to trust the Lord to meet their needs or to learn about Him and His ways. For forty years they wandered in the desert before they were in a position to enter the Promised Land. One of the recurring features of the Israelites' rebellion on this, and other occasions, was a demand to go back to Egypt (e.g. see Exodus 17:3, Numbers 11:20, 14:2-4).

## The corresponding danger for Jewish Christians

The parallel danger for these Jewish Christians was that they would turn away from Jesus as their Messiah and go back to Judaism. They, like the Israelites of Moses' day, had seen the Lord in action – through the death and resurrection of the Lord Jesus and also in the actions of the apostles during the Acts period, which were characterised by signs and wonders. So Hebrews 3:12-14 urges them not to have an unbelieving heart that turns away from the living God. Verse 14 echoes the warning of verse 6:

| Passage | The Hebrews' Position | The condition |
|---------|----------------------|---------------|
| Hebrews 3:6 | We are his house | if we hold on to our courage and the hope of which we boast |
| Hebrews 3:14 | We have come to share in Christ | if we hold firmly to the end the confidence we had at first. |

There is a similar idea here to the Lord Jesus' teaching in John 15 about "remaining in Him." He says:

> "Remain in me, and I will remain in you. No branch can bear fruit by itself; it must remain in the vine. Neither can you bear fruit unless you remain in me ... As the Father has loved me, so have I loved you. Now remain in my love. If you obey my commands you will remain in my love, just as I have obeyed my Father's commands and remain in his love." (John 15:4, 9-10)

*An application to the present*

In the twenty-first century we face similar temptations to turn back from following the Lord. Jesus told His disciples that they needed to love Him and show that love by obeying His commands (primarily the command to love one another) in order to remain in Him. It's not easy to keep going, to progress in our knowledge of God and to hold firmly to the enthusiasm we had in the beginning. Hebrews 3:13 warns us about sin's deceitfulness and teaches us to encourage one another on a daily basis. Following the Lord involves a day by day discipline, which is why Hebrews 3:15 warns these Jewish believers in the words of Psalm 95 – today, in the here and now, do not allow sin to deceive you into hardening your hearts, as your forefathers did.

*The danger re-emphasised*

Hebrews 3 then concludes, in verses 16-18 with three questions that highlight the reality of the danger these Jewish Christians faced:

1. Who was it who heard and rebelled? It was the very people who had been led out of Egypt and had witnessed the Lord's work among them.
2. Who was God angry with for forty years? It was those same people who sinned against Him and who died in the wilderness.
3. To whom did God swear that they would never enter His rest? Those same people who had disobeyed Him.

These Israelites who followed Moses had been delivered from Egypt and had seen God in action, yet because of their unbelief God was angry with them and condemned them to spend their lives wandering in the desert rather than moving into the land that had been promised. It was even more significant for those who had tasted of the heavenly gift, who had shared in the Holy Spirit, if they fell away from following the Lord Jesus. God's self-revelation through Christ was even clearer than His revelation through Moses. Therefore, turning back from following Him was an even more serious problem.

Because of their unbelief, that generation of Israelites who came out of Egypt were unable to enter the rest God promised them. In their case, this was the land of Canaan, where they would find peace, freedom and their needs would be met. Moses, because of his own failure (see Numbers 20:12) was unable to lead the people into the land and he, too, died in the desert. The privilege of leading the people into their rest went to Joshua, who, decades earlier, had been one of the spies who had given a favourable report on Israel's ability to take the land.

But the rest for the Israelites was a picture of a much more wonderful rest which is available to the Lord's people in Christ. The next section of Hebrews develops the issues that were raised in chapter 3 and demonstrates the superiority of the Lord Jesus to Joshua.

# The Son's superiority to Joshua

# The Son's superiority to Joshua
# Hebrews 4:1-13

The warnings in chapter 3 are repeated in chapter 4 and again they are linked with the "rest" for the people of God. As in chapter 3 the writer refers to Psalm 95. Chapter 4 begins with a statement that the promise of entering His rest still stands but that these Hebrew Christians need to be careful in case they, like the unfaithful Israelites, fall short and do not enter into that rest. The trouble was that, although the message was preached to those who came out of Egypt, it had no value because, as verse 2 says, "those who heard did not combine it with faith." There is, however, a marginal reading contained in many manuscripts that says, "they did not share in the faith of those who obeyed."

There is therefore a suggestion that those who did believe and trust did enter into that "rest". The Israelites wandered for forty years in the desert and that entire faithless generation died without entering the land. The only exceptions were Caleb and Joshua who, alone, believed that the Israelites would be able to conquer the promised land with God's help.

*A future rest for the people of God*

In verses 3, 5 and 8 Hebrews 4 quotes Psalm 95, repeating the Lord's judgment on that generation of Israel, that they would not enter the land. The Psalmist warned his contemporaries not to harden their hearts, as their ancestors had done. Therefore,

Hebrews argues, since this was written long after the Exodus period, it shows that David had in mind a future rest for his readers. It is interesting that, although Psalm 95 warns against hardening their hearts, this future rest is not explicitly mentioned in the psalm, but is inferred by the writer to the Hebrews.

Therefore, Hebrews continues, the rest offered by Joshua really points to a further, greater rest for God's people – that provided by Jesus the Messiah. This is described in verse 9 as a "Sabbath-rest for the people of God," as everyone who enters that rest will rest from their work, just as God rested from His, on the seventh day of creation.

**What is the "rest" – salvation or reward?**

What was it that these faithless Israelites forfeited and what is it that these Hebrew Christians are in danger of falling short of (verse 1)? Is it salvation that is in mind, or something else? If we consider the Israelites who died in the wilderness without entering the Promised Land, it seems unreasonable to suggest that they were all "lost" as we would understand the term. If so, it would include Moses and Aaron, who were among that group who did not enter the land. This would appear to be extremely unlikely, to say the least, particularly since Moses appeared on the mountain of transfiguration with the Lord (Luke 9:28-36) and is numbered among the giants of faith, who are discussed in Hebrews 11. So the rest must mean something other than salvation.

Welch and Allen point out that

> ... the grand exhortation of Hebrews is to "go on to perfection," perfection being the doctrinal equivalent of "the rest that remaineth" ... That rest that remaineth unto the people of God is a rest which follows completed work

... Sabbath *succeeding* work is not gospel, *it is reward*. "Let us labour, therefore," while at the same time rest in the finished work of Christ. (Charles Welch and Stuart Allen *Perfection or Perdition*, p203, emphasis in the original)

In keeping with the theme of the epistle, then, the rest does not refer to salvation. Unlike salvation it is something that we can fail to attain to. It therefore must relate to a reward for faithfulness to the Lord.

## How do they enter the "rest"?

One requirement for gaining that rest for those to whom the epistle was written, was to believe the gospel (Hebrews 4:3), but at the same time they were being urged to "make every effort to enter that rest" (verse 11). As also indicated by Welch and Allen's comment quoted above, something more than simply believing in Jesus was required; there was also the need for "labour" or "effort" to last the course. This point can also be illustrated from the experience of the Israelites in the wilderness. They did not enter Joshua's rest because "they did not share in the faith of those who obeyed," (verse 2, alternative rendering) and also because of their disobedience (verses 6 and 11). Lack of faithful obedience seems to have been the problem. The Israelites of old vacillated between following the Lord and rebelling against Him. When He showed His power, either in blessing (e.g. Exodus 14:31) or in punishing (e.g. Numbers 21:7), they vowed their allegiance to Him. However, when things went wrong, they quickly became discouraged and grumbled (e.g. Exodus 15:23-24), threatening to go back to Egypt (e.g. Numbers 14:2-4).

*The need for unwavering trust*

What the Lord wanted from the Israelites was a steady unwavering trust in His ability and willingness to lead them into their rest – the Promised Land - and He also wanted to see the obedience that resulted from such a trust. They, however, refused to follow Joshua and Caleb's example in this and died in the desert as a result. These Hebrew Christians were being urged to "leave the elementary teachings about Christ and go on to maturity," (Hebrews 6:1). This mature faith – a faith that is steadfast and consistent and lived out genuinely and without tainted motives - is what the Lord wants from His children. As suggested in the previous chapter, the Israelites in the wilderness faced the temptation not to go forward but to return to Egypt, while the readers of Hebrews faced a similar temptation to revert to Judaism, as the persecution of believers and the rigours of authentic Christian living began to bite.

For us living 2,000 years later, the temptations may be different – perhaps to soft-pedal our faith, or compromise our beliefs or conduct, to accommodate the views and behaviour of our own contemporaries; perhaps not to take our Christian beliefs seriously enough to make a significant difference to the kind of people we are. If we are to go on to maturity, gain our reward and enter into our rest, we cannot have that attitude. What the Lord is looking for is an uncompromising faith that obeys Him and trusts Him for the outcome. This is the way by which we can enter into the rest promised by the Lord Jesus, which is vastly superior to the limited rest offered by Joshua to the Israelites.

Although Christians are saved by their faith in the completed work of Christ and there is no condemnation to those who are in Christ Jesus, we all will have to give an account of ourselves, our lives and our service before Him. This is a very sobering thought and the final two verses of this section set the facts before us.

## The Word of God as a revealer of thoughts (Hebrews 4:12-13)

God, as Paul observes in Galatians 6:7, cannot be mocked; we reap exactly what we sow. The Word of God – best understood here as the teaching of Scripture rather than the Lord Jesus Himself – is like a sword with the power to cut through flesh and bone at a stroke and lay bare the thoughts and attitudes of the heart (Hebrews 4:12). In fact, it is sharper than a sword. If we come face to face with the Scriptures, they will reveal to us what we are truly like and we will stand exposed.

Worse, this exposure will be before the eyes of the One to whom we have to give an account of ourselves (verse 13). There is no escape; there can be no pretence or excuses; everything will be out in the open, before His gaze.

Yet this exposure to the Word of God is not necessarily only a future event. As we read His Word on a daily basis and take it to heart, this exposure of our true selves can give us perspective. It may be painful at times but the Holy Spirit, working within us, can transform our lives to bring them into line with His purposes, developing our trusting obedience to Him.

James talks of the impact the Scriptures can have on someone who studies them, but only if they are taken seriously.

> Do not merely listen to the word, and so deceive yourselves. Do what it says. Anyone who listens to the word but does not do what it says is like a man who looks

at his face in a mirror and after looking at himself, goes away and immediately forgets what he looks like. But the man who looks intently into the perfect law that gives freedom, and continues to do this, not forgetting what he has heard, but doing it – he will be blessed in what he does. (James 1:22-25)

But these Hebrews had another One who would be able to help them – a High Priest who is able to sympathise with their weaknesses and can represent them before God – and His priesthood is infinitely superior to that of Aaron. This is the subject of the next section.

# The Son's superiority to Aaron

# The Son's superiority to Aaron
# Hebrews 4:14-7:28

This major section of Hebrews carefully sets out the superiority of Christ's priesthood to the Aaronic, Levitical priesthood, which, together with the Law that went with it, had been superseded. This was another extremely sensitive area for the Jewish readers. So the arguments are laid out in detail, extensively supported by quotations from the Psalms.

## A high priest who can sympathise with mankind (Hebrews 4:14-5:3)

Since we are all exposed to God's gaze it is fortunate that we have One who can represent us before Him. Hebrews 4:14-15 introduces "Jesus the Son of God" (verse 14) as a great high priest, who represents His people, not on the earth, as Aaron did, but in the presence of God in heaven. Right away we can see the superiority of His priesthood.

The first three verses of chapter 5 explain that a high priest is appointed from among his people to represent them. He can sympathise with them because he has experienced the same difficulties, weaknesses and temptations that they have. That is why he has to offer sacrifices not only for their sin but also for his own.

But how can such a glorious One as "Jesus, Son of God" truly represent us? Hebrews 4:15 explains that He is not so remote from us that He cannot sympathise with our weaknesses because He has experienced them Himself. As Hebrews 2:17 points out, Jesus was "made like his brothers in every way." He was tempted like us but the essential difference was that, unlike Aaron and the other priests who followed him, He never yielded to these temptations (4:15).

As a result we are able to approach God's throne with confidence (4:16) because we find that it is a throne of grace, rather than judgment, and there we can receive mercy and grace to help us, rather than condemnation.

"But," a Jewish reader might object, "How could Jesus be a priest? He was from the tribe of Judah, not Levi. Judah was the tribe of kings not priests. Besides, He can't just appoint Himself as a priest."

Hebrews now goes on to answer these objections. The Lord Jesus is not a self-appointed priest. He was called by God to the position (5:4). Furthermore, the Lord Jesus' priesthood is not a continuation of the Levitical priesthood. He is a priest of an entirely different order – the order of Melchizedek, and He, like Melchizedek, filled the dual role of king and priest.

## The qualifications of Jesus for the priesthood (Hebrews 5:4-10)

Like Aaron, Jesus was appointed as a priest by God. To prove this the writer refers again to two Psalms - Psalms 2 and 110.

First he quotes Psalm 2 to show the fitness of Christ for the position of high priest.

> You are my Son; today I have become your Father. (Hebrews 5:5)

His fitness is demonstrated by the fact that He is the Son of God, but His actual call to the priesthood comes in a quote from Psalm 110.

> You are a priest forever, in the order of Melchizedek. (Hebrews 5:6)

Both of these Psalms have already been quoted in Hebrews 1 in the context of Christ's superiority to angels. Psalm 2 reveals God addressing the king of Israel as His Son. Psalm 110 shows that God has also called Him to be a priest in the order of Melchizedek.

This is the first of eight mentions of Melchizedek in Hebrews. He is dealt with in more detail in chapter 7 but here the writer introduces him briefly. Melchizedek, like Jesus, was both priest and king – two offices which were never elsewhere combined in Israel in Old Testament times.

The fitness of Jesus to be priest is also demonstrated by the fact that He learned obedience through what He suffered. Hebrews 5:7-9 describe the Lord Jesus' experience of His own weakness, crying out to God for deliverance. It appears that Gethsemane is in mind here, when the Lord pleaded for the cup He was about to drink to be taken from Him. However, as verse 7 tells us, He reverently submitted to the Father's will and, as a result, became the source of eternal salvation for all believers (verse 9). Although He was the Son of God, He had to *learn* obedience; He had to experience being torn between the desire to follow His own interests and the need to do His Father's will. Through the choice He made, He was made "perfect" (verse 9). In other words, He reached the full maturity of a true Son of the Father. Because of His experience, He is able to sympathise with us and help us when we are faced with similar dilemmas, although, obviously, our temptations can never be as extreme as His.

Because of the experiences He came through, as verse 10 shows, He was designated a priest in the order, not of Aaron, but of Melchizedek.

## Interlude: An exhortation and an encouragement (Hebrews 5:11-6:20)

The writer has two major points to make before he explores the nature of the Melchizedek priesthood in depth. Firstly, realising that what he is about to say has profound implications, he urges his readers in 5:11-6:12 to progress beyond the basic teachings about Christ and to go on to maturity, to grapple with the deep truths that he is about to discuss.

A sad characteristic of the Lord's people throughout their history has been a reluctance to leave the "milk" of elementary truth and move on to the "solid food" of mature doctrine, which, as 5:14 points out, is necessary if they are going to be able to distinguish good and evil. These then are serious issues. His readers have to apply their minds to what is to come, because understanding the truths that are about to be revealed is critical to their growth towards maturity.

Secondly, in 6:13-20, he tries to emphasise the trustworthiness of the information he is about to explain. That trustworthiness is based on the unchanging nature of God's promises. Since God cannot lie, those who are trusting in His promises can take great encouragement (6:18). Hebrews 6:13 indicates that God made His promise to Abraham. He also confirmed that promise with an oath so that those to whom the promise was made (Abraham and his seed) would realise the unchanging nature of what was promised (verse 17).

By this double guarantee – a promise supported by an oath, both made by the One who cannot lie – God is saying with all the power at His command that there is no uncertainty about what He is promising. In fact, as verses 19-20 indicate, their hope in His promises is like a great anchor, linked with an unbreakable cord that reaches right into heaven, where the great high priest has gone.

So what is the hope that is so sure and certain? It is the hope in the effectiveness and permanence of His priesthood in the order of Melchizedek (verse 20). Chapter 7 is about to demonstrate that this priesthood has superseded the Aaronic priesthood, the Law of Moses that accompanied it and the old covenant that formed the framework for the whole system. No wonder the writer pauses to encourage and reassure his readers. He is now leading them into uncharted waters.

## Melchizedek, Priest and King (Hebrews 7:1-10)

*Who was Melchizedek?*

Melchizedek appears in only one Old Testament passage – Genesis 14:17-20. After Abram returned from defeating the kings who had kidnapped Lot and his family, he was met by Melchizedek, king of Salem (i.e. what is now Jerusalem), who is described as "priest of God Most High" (Genesis 14:18). Melchizedek, then, was both priest and king. Melchizedek blessed both Abram and the Lord, who had enabled Abram to win the battle and rescue his nephew. He also presented Abram with bread and wine and after this, Abram gave him a tithe (i.e. a tenth) "of everything" (verse 20).

Hebrews 7:1-3 gives us more information about Melchizedek:

- His name itself means "king of righteousness" and his title "king of Salem" means "king of peace" (verse 2). Such titles remind us of the Lord Jesus Christ.

- He is described as being "without father or mother, without genealogy, without beginning of days or end of life" (verse 3).

- He is therefore like the Son of God – a priest forever (verse 3).

The latter two points have led some writers to suggest that Melchizedek was really immortal and even that he was Jesus in human form. This is very unlikely and Hebrews is probably only saying that no one knows where he came from or where he went.

Nevertheless, the perpetual nature of his priesthood and the fact that, unlike the Aaronic priesthood, it was not subject to succession, is critical to the argument of the next section of the epistle – to show that Christ's priesthood, like that of Melchizedek, is better than that of Aaron.

*The superiority of the Melchizedek priesthood to that of Aaron*

In verses 5-10 the writer gives four reasons for the superiority of the Melchizedek priesthood. The arguments are not always clear for Western minds to follow but together they form a formidable case. The four reasons are:

- Under the Law the Levitical priests were paid tithes *by* the rest of the Israelite people, Abraham's descendants. But Abraham paid a tithe *to* Melchizedek, who was not even descended from Levi. (verses 5-6)

- Melchizedek blessed Abraham, the man to whom God's promises had been made. Since the lesser is always blessed by the greater, this shows that Melchizedek was greater than Abraham. (verses 6-7)

- The Levitical priests were all subject to death but the great priest in the order of Melchizedek lives forever, as Psalm 110:4 states. (verse 8)

- Levi, who normally *collected* the tithe from his brothers, *paid* the tithe through Abraham to Melchizedek, because as he was unborn at the time of Abraham, he could be metaphorically viewed as still being in the body of Abraham. (verses 9-10)

The priesthood of Melchizedek, then, was better than the Aaronic priesthood ministered by the Levites. The Lord Jesus Christ – the great priest-king in the order of Melchizedek, who is a priest forever – is not dependent on succession because He lives forever and His priesthood is permanent (7:24).

Hebrews 7 has more to say about the nature of this great priest when it discusses the replacement of the old covenant by a new covenant. However, before we come to that, we have to consider the place of the Law, which was bound up with the Levitical priesthood. If the priesthood is superseded by something greater, what is to happen to the Law?

## The order of Melchizedek and the Law (Hebrews 7:11-19)

The connection between the Levitical priesthood and the Law is perhaps a surprising one: verse 11 indicates that the Law was given on the basis of the priesthood. It might have been expected to be the other way round. But it is clear that the priesthood had priority.

*The failure of the Levitical system*

The sacrificial system that surrounded the priesthood was the way in which God taught the Israelites that sacrifice was necessary for the remission of sin. These sacrifices, of course, did not actually achieve cleansing for the people, as Hebrews 10:3 points out:

> Those sacrifices are an annual reminder of sins, because it is impossible for the blood of bulls and goats to take away sins.

They pointed towards the truly effective sacrifice that was to come. The Law, similarly, functioned to make people aware of their failings and bring them to Christ, as Paul explains in Galatians 3.

What, then, was the purpose of the law? It was added because of transgressions until the Seed to whom the promise referred had come ... So the law was put in charge to lead us to Christ that we might be justified by faith. Now that faith has come, we are no longer under the supervision of the law. (Galatians 3:19, 24-25)

The Levitical priesthood and the Law pointed forward to Christ and Hebrews 7:11 makes the point that if these could have brought perfection (or completeness) then there would have been no need for another priest, of a different order, to be revealed. But when the old priesthood was superseded, so was the Law that went with it (verse 12).

The problem with the priesthood and its Law was that they were "weak and useless" and the Law made nothing perfect (verse 19). Again we have echoes of Paul's letter to the Galatians:

For if a law had been given that could impart life, then righteousness would certainly have come by the law. (Galatians 3:21)

But the Law could not give life; the annually repeated sacrifices could not bring cleansing; the position of humanity appeared hopeless. They had been made aware of their failings, but given no means of overcoming them. However, they were not lost because the Levitical system pointed forward to a new and better priesthood, described in verse 19 as:

... a better hope ... by which we draw near to God.

In explaining this idea of a better hope, the writer in verses 13-17 focuses again on Melchizedek's priesthood, its differences from the Levitical priesthood and its superiority to it.

First, it is clear that this priesthood is under an entirely different regime. As was mentioned earlier, the Lord Jesus came from the tribe of Judah and Moses said nothing about priests coming from that tribe (verse 14), so Jesus' priesthood had nothing to do with Moses or the law. Apart from Melchizedek, only Christ is both priest and king. Psalm 110 introduces Messiah in these two positions. Zechariah 6:12-13 also confirms this unique situation:

> Tell him this is what the Lord Almighty says: "Here is the man whose name is the Branch, and he will branch out from his place and build the temple of the Lord ... and he will be clothed with majesty and will sit and rule on his throne. And he will be a priest on his throne. And there will be harmony between the two."

But the important issue is the nature of the priest. He, like Melchizedek, appears without genealogy (Hebrews 7:3), so He has become a priest, not on the basis of His family succession, like the Levites, but on the basis of the "power of an indestructible life" (verse 16). To prove this, the writer again quotes Psalm 110 in Hebrews 7:17. Jesus is a priest forever! Because of this, God's people are no longer locked into a system that cannot give completeness and final consummation. Instead, they are being represented in God's very presence by the One whose priesthood will never end. As the writer said at the end of chapter 6:

> We have this hope as an anchor for the soul, firm and secure. It enters the inner sanctuary behind the curtain, where Jesus, who went before us, has entered on our behalf. (Hebrews 6:19-20)

# A permanent priesthood confirmed by an oath (Hebrews 7:20-28)

This final section concludes the discussion on the superiority of Christ's priesthood. To some extent the writer is going over old ground and recapping on points he has made earlier but he takes his earlier arguments further and prepares the way for what is to come – the discussion of the new covenant. In these 9 verses there are three distinct points being made.

1. *Christ was appointed a priest by an oath of God (verses 20-21).*

Other priests were not so appointed. And yet again Psalm 110:4 is quoted to support this assertion. This is not the first time God's oath has been mentioned. In Hebrews 6, the certainty of God's promise was indicated by the fact that it was confirmed by an oath. Here, however, the writer takes the matter further by stating in verse 22 that:

> Because of this oath, Jesus has become the guarantee of a better covenant.

As he did with Melchizedek, the writer briefly introduces the new covenant before going on to discuss it in more detail in chapter 8. This is the first mention of the word "covenant" in Hebrews, which is perhaps surprising, given that it is such a key word for the Jewish people. But what is really important is to note that Jesus is described as the "guarantee" of a better covenant. He is not just the mediator of the new covenant, he is the guarantee that it will be fulfilled. And verses 23-25 show the way in which he guarantees this covenant.

*2. Christ has a permanent priesthood (verses 23-25).*

The mortality of other priests means that they cannot continue indefinitely in office. But because the Lord Jesus lives forever, He can save His people completely because He is always there in God's presence, to make intercession for them. Their future glory is assured.

*3. Christ, the high priest is pure and blameless (verses 26-28).*

Verse 26 spells out the glory of Christ; He is "holy, blameless, pure, set apart from sinners, exalted above the heavens" and therefore completely able to meet the priestly needs of mankind. But these characteristics also illustrate one final aspect of the superiority of His priesthood to that of Aaron. Unlike the Levitical priests, who were flawed men, He did not need to offer sacrifices for His own sin as well as the sins of the people. Instead, He sacrificed *Himself* for their sins, once and for all – a totally effectual sacrifice – something that bulls and goats could never achieve.

So the climax is reached. The priesthood of the Lord Jesus Christ is infinitely superior to the Aaronic priesthood administered by the Levites. This section of Hebrews has identified several ways in which the Lord's priesthood is superior. These are:

- Unlike the Levitical priests, He combines the offices of priest and king.

- He does not minister as a priest on earth but in the presence of God in heaven.

- Although He was tempted in all ways like us, yet He was without sin, unlike the Levitical priests.

- He is a priest in the order of Melchizedek, who was recognised in the Old Testament as being greater than Abraham, and, therefore, Levi.

- He is without genealogy, so His is not a priesthood on the basis of succession. Instead He is a priest on the basis of an indestructible life. He therefore has a permanent priesthood since He is not subject to death.

- Unlike other priests, He was appointed by an oath and a promise of God.

- Other priests sacrificed repeatedly and their sacrifices were not truly effective. Christ's sacrifice was once for all and it was completely effective at removing sin because it was the sacrifice of Himself, the spotless lamb of God.

So Hebrews has established the superiority of the priesthood of Christ. It has superseded the Levitical priesthood and the Law that went along with it. But if these have been replaced, what has taken their place? In Hebrews 7:22 we read of the "better covenant", one which had long been predicted but was now being introduced by the Lord Jesus. This is the subject of chapter 8 of the epistle.

# The Son as the guarantee of a superior covenant

# The Son as the guarantee of a superior covenant
# Hebrews 8:1-13

Hebrews 7:22 introduces the idea of a covenant for the first time. There is a link between covenant and priesthood. Hebrews 7:21 states that the Lord Jesus is a priest forever and that this is confirmed by an oath from God. Because of this, verse 22 says, Jesus is the guarantor of a better covenant. Hebrews 8 now discusses the nature of this "new covenant" and its superiority to the "old covenant."

A covenant is an agreement between two parties - often between a king and his subjects, whereby the king will make promises to his people and the people will agree to support the king and follow him. There are several covenants in the Old Testament between God and His people but in this section of Hebrews the term "old covenant" is used to describe the Sinai covenant and "new covenant" to describe the covenant proclaimed by Jeremiah 31:31-34.

# A better ministry in a better tabernacle
## (Hebrews 8:1-6)

Chapter 8 opens with a statement of the superiority of the ministry of Christ. These Jewish Christians have already learned (in Hebrews 4:14) that they have a high priest who has gone through the heavens and who ministers there rather, than on the earth, as the Levitical priests did. Now this is picked up again at the start of chapter 8. Christ the high priest has sat down at the right hand of God and serves there, in the true tabernacle, rather than on earth in the original tabernacle.

It is interesting that Christ is described as being seated. This suggests that His sacrificial work is completed. The Levitical priests *stand*, day after day, administering the same sacrifices over and over again, which can never effectively take away sins (Hebrews 10:11). Christ's sacrificial work, by contrast, is a once and for all sacrifice which is completed and is effectual. The nature of that sacrifice is discussed in detail in chapter 9. The Lord's service at the present time (8:2) is one of intercession for us before the throne of grace (Hebrews 4:16).

The place where the Lord ministers is described in Hebrews 8:2 as being the "true tabernacle set up by the Lord," in contrast to the tabernacle set up by man. This tabernacle is not a "true" as opposed to a "false" tabernacle, but is in contrast to one which was only a picture of the real thing. The tabernacle on earth was a "copy and a shadow of what is in heaven" (Hebrews 8:5). "True" is also used of the Lord Jesus in this sense in John 1:9, where He is described as the "true light," and in John 15:1, where he calls Himself the "true vine."

When the people of Israel were wandering in the wilderness, God gave Moses detailed instructions for the building of the tabernacle, including the lampstand, the altar and all the priestly garments connected with it (see Exodus chapters 25-31). The instructions were very specific and Hebrews 8:5 tells us that Moses was

> ... warned when he was about to build the tabernacle: "See to it that you make everything according to the pattern shown you on the mountain."

The tabernacle built by Moses, though only a copy of the "true" tabernacle in heaven, had to be constructed with great care. Some have suggested that Moses actually was given a vision of the heavenly tabernacle, which he was to copy, when he was on the mountain (see e.g. Exodus 25:40). However, it is not certain that this should be taken literally. What is clear, though, is that the ministry of the glorified Lord Jesus in the true tabernacle, is superior to the ministry in the earthly tabernacle, just as the covenant of which He is mediator is superior to the old covenant (verse 6), because it is based on better promises (Hebrews 8:6).

## The superiority of the new covenant
## (Hebrews 8:7-13)

The writer now goes on to compare the new covenant with the old. He begins by making the point that if there had been no problems with the old covenant there would have been no need for a new one. So what was wrong with it? Verse 8 indicates that the fault lay with the people.

The difficulty was that the people were not able to keep the conditions of the old covenant, in spite of all their good intentions

(Exodus 24:3). The system of the old covenant served only to point out their sin to them, but was unable to cleanse them. As Paul explains in Romans 7, the law, although holy, righteous and good, was only able to bring sin into focus. As a result:

> I found that the very commandment that was intended to bring life actually brought death. (Romans 7:10)

It was the weakness of fallen humanity that caused the failure. Not only so, but the sacrificial system administered by the Levitical priests could not achieve real cleansing. All that was being offered was a figurative cleansing. Something more was needed. The writer is here building his case towards chapters 9 and 10. There he demonstrates that, just as Christ is the superior priest, so too is His sacrifice vastly superior to that of the Levitical system because it actually provides real cleansing from sin.

The new covenant, though, was not something introduced as an afterthought in the New Testament. It had been revealed some 600 years earlier through the prophet Jeremiah. In Hebrews 8:8-12 we have an extensive quotation from Jeremiah 31:31-34. The key features of the new covenant, contained in these verses are:

- It will be between the Lord and the houses of Judah and Israel. (verse 8)

- It will be different from the old covenant, since that one ended in failure when the people did not remain faithful to it and the Lord turned away from them. (verse 9)

- It will be made at a future date (from the date Jeremiah wrote). (verses 8, 10)

- God's law will be written on their hearts rather than on tablets of stone. (verse 10)

- The Lord will be their God and they will be His people. (verse 10)

- There will be no need for anyone to teach because all the people will know the Lord. (verse 11)

- Their sins will be permanently forgiven. (verse 12)

From these key points we can see the ways in which the new covenant will succeed where the old one failed: if God's law is written on their hearts, they will be pleased to obey, rather than be prone to fail; because they continue to follow the Lord, He will not turn away from them, but will be their God; the new covenant also accomplishes genuine, permanent forgiveness of sins, which could not be achieved under the old order.

Jeremiah, of course, was not the only one to envisage these days of glory. Ezekiel's vision of the valley of dry bones in chapter 37 was a picture of the future gathering together of the two houses of Israel as a single people. Ezekiel concludes:

> My dwelling place will be with them; I will be their God and they will be my people. Then the nations will know that I the Lord make Israel holy. (Ezekiel 37:27-28)

Similar words are used in Jeremiah of the implementation of the new covenant.

I will put my law in their minds and write it on their hearts. I will be their God and they will be my people. (Jeremiah 31:33)

The implementation of the new covenant is the way the Lord will make Israel holy, and the nations will note the fact. It is clear, therefore, that this vision for the future relates to a literal, natural Israel. For a discussion of the timing of the introduction of the new covenant, see *The New Covenant: Who is it with? When is it for?* by Michael Penny.[1]

Paul also, in his magnificent exposition of the future of Israel in Romans 9-11, finishes with the same triumphant conclusion, quoting Isaiah and Jeremiah to support his case:

> And so, all Israel will be saved, as it is written: "The deliverer will come from Zion; he will turn godlessness away from Jacob. And this is my covenant with them when I take away their sins." (Romans 11:26-27)

The old covenant, as Hebrews 8:13 tells us, has become obsolete and will soon disappear. This was a prophetic statement because in A.D.70, not long after these words were written, Israel rebelled against Rome and was destroyed as a nation. The temple – the heart of the Jewish religious system, was torn down as Jesus Himself had predicted in Matthew 24:2 and the survivors of the people scattered. But the message of the new covenant offered a sure and certain hope for the future.

The vision is totally breath-taking: the Levitical priesthood and the whole sacrificial system including the tabernacle, built to

---

[1] See page 97 for more on Covenants, in General, and the New Covenant, in particular.

God's instructions, all enshrined in the old covenant, had been unable to bring the people of Israel to God. However, now we read of a better priesthood, a true tabernacle, of which the tabernacle in the wilderness was only a poor shadow and a better covenant, which will enable the people of Israel to dwell with God and He with them. But how was this to be accomplished? The old covenant was implemented through a complex system of sacrifices. What is to take its place under the new covenant? The subject of sacrifice has been mentioned in chapters 7 and 8 but the writer is now going to explore it in depth in chapters 9 and 10.

# The Son as the provider of a superior sacrifice

# The Son as the provider of a superior sacrifice
# Hebrews 9:1-10:18

The author has already discussed the superiority of the Lord Jesus' priesthood to the Levitical priesthood and the superiority of the new covenant to the old. Now he turns his attention to the tabernacle and the sacrifices that belonged to the old administration to show their limitations. Although they were ordained by God for the people of Israel in the past, they were really ineffective in providing true cleansing from sins and in bringing people into fellowship with a holy God.

The tabernacle into which Christ entered, is, by contrast, infinitely more glorious. His sacrifice of Himself brought true forgiveness of sins and enabled man's relationship with God, which had been lost at the fall of Adam, to be restored.

First, however, the writer explains some features of the original sacrificial system in order to contrast it with the new.

## The original tabernacle and its limitations (Hebrews 9:1-10)

The first five verses of the chapter describe the tabernacle in some detail; the outer room, described as the Holy Place (verse 2), was where the priests ministered on a regular basis. The inner room, the Most Holy Place (verse 3), was only entered by the high priest once a year on the Day of Atonement. He went into the Most Holy Place to present the blood of the sacrifice, first for his own sins and then for the sins of the people. However, these sacrifices could only cleanse the people from ceremonial contamination, not from moral guilt (verse 10). They did not reach the conscience of the people (verse 9). This is a very important issue and the point is repeated in verse 13.

> The blood of goats and bulls and the ashes of a heifer sprinkled on those who are ceremonially unclean sanctify them so that they are outwardly clean. (Hebrews 9:13)

This very limited cleansing from ceremonial contamination enabled the people to live in the community of Israel but what was to be done about their moral failings?

The system surrounding the original tabernacle had other limitations too. The fact that only the high priest could go through the curtain into the Most Holy Place showed that there was still a barrier between God and man. How could it be otherwise since the people's sins had not been removed? While the old order was still functioning, a way of access had not been revealed (verse 8). Not only that, but the high priest had to go in year after year to carry out the same ceremony, which shows that it was not permanently effective (10:1-2).

However, recognising the limitations in the ceremonies connected with the old covenant could enable the Hebrew believers to see even more clearly the complete perfection of the new order introduced by the Lord Jesus.

# The superiority of the Lord Jesus' sacrifice
# (Hebrews 9:11-14)

Hebrews chapter 9 indicates four ways in which the sacrifice of Christ was superior to the sacrifices under the old covenant.

## 1. *The tabernacle He entered was superior (9:11)*

The Lord Jesus, the great high priest, did not enter the earthly tabernacle, but the heavenly – the tabernacle of which the earthly tabernacle was only a "copy and shadow of what is in heaven" (8:5). This was "the true tabernacle set up by the Lord, not by man" (8:2).

## 2. *The Lord entered the heavenly tabernacle once for all (9:12)*

In contrast to the Levitical high priest, who entered the Most Holy Place year after year, the Lord Jesus entered the heavenly tabernacle only once (9:25). When He did so, He did not immediately come out, as the Levitical high priest did, to prove to the people that his sacrifice had been accepted. Instead, having offered one sacrifice for sins, He sat down at the right hand of God (10:12). This contrast is brought out in Hebrews 8:1-2, where the seated Lord Jesus, as high priest, is described as *remaining* in the sanctuary to serve.

## 3. *The Lord offered His own blood, not the blood of animals (9:12-13)*

This is an extremely startling statement. The Israelites had to provide animals for sacrifice which were without physical defect and their blood provided ceremonial cleansing. The Lord Jesus, on the other hand, offered His own blood as a sacrifice.

The lesson that God had taught the Israelites by the repeated ceremonies was that there could be no cleansing from sin without the shedding of blood and the giving of a life (9:22). But here was a sacrifice on an entirely different level and the reference to the Lord's blood highlights the fourth aspect of its superiority.

4. *The sacrifice of the Lord Jesus, unlike the animal sacrifices, was effective in removing moral guilt (9:14)*

This is the real crux of the matter. The sacrifice of Christ enables the believer to be cleansed from the moral guilt stemming from the sin that has condemned mankind to death since the Fall. We are sinners by nature and by practice, but the sacrifice of Christ on the cross removed our sin and guilt and restored our relationship with God.

When the Lord Jesus died on the cross, Matthew 27:51 tells us that:

> At that moment the curtain of the temple was torn in two from top to bottom.

The curtain, the barrier which had separated God and man, had been removed. It is interesting to notice that the curtain was torn from the top down. The initiative came from the Father, not from man.

It is important to remember that the sacrifice of the Lord on the cross was not His own idea; it was the Father's plan to accomplish the reconciliation of man to God. As Denney says:

> Atonement is not something contrived, as it were, behind the Father's back; it is the Father's way of making it possible for the sinful to have fellowship with Him. (James Denney, *The Death of Christ*, p122)

As we have seen, the Lord Jesus was *sent by God* into the world to speak to mankind in a more direct way than ever before (Hebrews 1:1-2); the Lord Jesus was *appointed by God* as a priest in the order of Melchizedek (Hebrews 5:5-6); the Lord Jesus *learned obedience as a son* from what He suffered (Hebrews 5:8). The initiative lay with the Father, who, in His grace and mercy, worked out His plan of reconciliation.

But what made the sacrifice of Christ so effective when animal sacrifices were not?

## The effectiveness of the Lord Jesus' sacrifice (Hebrews 9:14-28)

In this passage we are not told how the sacrifice of Christ is effective in securing our salvation, but a couple of clues as to the critical factors are given to us in Hebrews 9:14. Firstly, the Lord Jesus was *unblemished*, not in the outward, physical sense of the animals which were sacrificed, but in His very nature. He became man, but, being the Son of God, He did not have the inner contamination that causes us to be biased towards doing what is wrong. Not only so, but He did not, Himself, commit sin during

His earthly life. He was morally and ethically spotless. By living out His 33 years on earth in this way He was able to succeed where Adam and all his descendants failed.

Secondly, He offered Himself *voluntarily* to fulfil God's will by being the perfect sacrifice. He was not a non-consenting or ignorant victim; He went to the cross in the full understanding of what it entailed and, though in Gethsemane He was almost overwhelmed by the enormity of what lay before Him, He went voluntarily to the cross. When Peter tried to defend Him in Gethsemane His response showed that He could have backed out of the situation at any time but, if He had done so, how would the Father's purposes be fulfilled?

> Do you think I cannot call on my Father, and he will at once put at my disposal more than twelve legions of angels? But how then would the Scriptures be fulfilled that say it must happen in this way? (Matthew 26:53-54)

In his Christian allegory *The Lion, the Witch and the Wardrobe*, C. S. Lewis also picks up on these two points identified in Hebrews 9:14. When Aslan, the Christ figure in the story, is raised to life, he explains to the two children how this was possible. The witch was very clever but her knowledge only went back to the dawn of time:

> But if she could have looked a little further back ... she would have known that when a willing victim who had committed no treachery was killed in a traitor's stead, the Table would crack and Death itself would start working backwards. (C. S. Lewis, *The Lion, the Witch and the Wardrobe*, p171)

We are dealing with a very deep mystery here. The key truth to recognise is what the author tells us in Hebrews 9:27-28:

> Just as man is destined to die once and after that to face judgment, so Christ was sacrificed once to take away the sins of many people; and he will appear a second time, not to bear sin, but to bring salvation to those who are waiting for him.

The Lord Jesus died on the cross but He did not face judgment. The fact that He was raised to incorruptible life showed that His sacrifice was accepted and because He lives, those of us who are in Him will live also. Therefore, when He comes a second time, it will not be to deal with sin – that has been cleansed once for all; it will be to usher in His kingdom and make salvation a living reality in space and time for His people.

*The covenant and the inheritance*

In verses 16-17 of Hebrews 9 the writer changes tack and starts to use the word "covenant" in the sense of a "will." The terms of a will can only be implemented on the death of the person who made the will (verses 16-17). This is why both the old and new covenants required the shedding of blood. Moses sprinkled the blood of the old covenant on the people (verse 19); the Lord Jesus' blood was shed to cleanse us from acts that lead to death (verse 14).

In Exodus 24:8 we read of Moses confirming the covenant between the Lord and the people of Israel:

> Moses then took the blood, sprinkled it on the people and said, "This is the blood of the covenant that the Lord has made with you in accordance with all these words."

The Lord Jesus, in His final meal with His disciples, spoke similar words to describe the new covenant that He was initiating, using wine as a symbol of His blood:

> This is my blood of the covenant, which is poured out for many for the forgiveness of sins. (Matthew 26:28)

But the beneficiaries of a will receive an inheritance and the death of Christ means that both those under the new and the old covenants can enter that inheritance.

> For this reason Christ is the mediator of a new covenant that those who are called may receive the promised eternal inheritance – now that he has died as a ransom to set them free from the sins committed under the first covenant. (Hebrews 9:15)

Here of course, we have the unique situation whereby Christ is the mediator or administrator of the will and also the One who died. Similarly, He is both the priest who administers the sacrifice under the new covenant and the sacrifice Himself. What a profound truth!

## A recapitulation (Hebrews 10:1-18)

In the first half of chapter 10, the author largely goes back over ground that has already been covered, emphasising the key points that have been made and adding further explanations and insights as he goes.

First, he reiterates the point made earlier that the Law was only a shadow of the good things that were coming. The sacrifices being offered under the old covenant could never be effective in cleansing from moral guilt. If they had been effective, then they would continue to be offered and there would be no need for something new (verse 2). However, since the blood of bulls and goats could not take away sins, they served only as a reminder of sins. What a miserable situation to be in! To have no means of achieving cleansing from sin, but constantly having to offer futile sacrifices, which kept the fact of your sin, and the guilt associated with it, constantly in front of your eyes.

But into this situation stepped the Lord Jesus Christ. In verses 5-7 the writer quotes another Messianic Psalm – Psalm 40. The speaker, identified in verse 5 as Christ, offers (again the idea of a willing victim) to submit Himself to God's will. The Psalm states that what God was really looking for was not sacrifices and offerings (verse 5); God was not pleased with these (verse 6), even though it was He Himself who had established the Law that required the sacrifices (verse 8). Instead, God's will and purpose was that His Son should come to earth as the real sacrifice to which the old covenant shadows pointed. So God prepared a body for Him (verse 5) that would enable this to be accomplished.

The recurring theme here is the voluntary nature of Christ's sacrifice. We find this stated in verse 7 in the quotation from Psalm 40, and then re-emphasised by the author in verse 9. As we have already seen in chapter 9, the Lord Jesus was never *forced* to go to the cross. He *chose* to go there voluntarily, so that the Scriptures would be fulfilled and His Father's purpose of reconciliation achieved. The contrast between verses 1 and 10 is really striking:

> The law is only a shadow of the good things that are coming – not the realities themselves. For this reason it can never, by the same sacrifices repeated endlessly year

after year, make perfect those who draw near to worship. (verse 1)

And by that will, we have been made holy through the sacrifice of the body of Jesus Christ once for all. (verse 10)

Still the author wants to emphasise the point further and in verses 11-12 he again describes the Levitical priest, standing and performing his sacrificial duties time after time, sacrifices that can never take away sins. Then he paints a picture of the great high priest, sitting down at the right hand of God, having made the one sacrifice for sins for all time:

... because by one sacrifice he has made perfect forever those who are being made holy. (verse 14)

The scope of the truth here is breathtaking. In one great sweep the writer has laid out before us the purpose of the ages. The old covenant with its priesthood, its Law and its sacrifices all eclipsed by the new covenant, with an eternal priesthood in the order of Melchizedek, with the Law abolished and with the one sacrifice of Christ achieving cleansing from sins and moral guilt for all time.

To remind us where the idea of a new covenant came from, the writer again quotes Jeremiah 31:33-34. This spoke of the day when the Lord would make a new covenant with the house of Israel and the house of Judah, when He would write His laws on their hearts, and would remember their iniquities no more. So, the author adds

Where these have been forgiven, there is no longer any sacrifice for sin. (verse 18)

The opening 9½ chapters of Hebrews have comprehensively explored the religious system of Israel and demonstrated the superiority of Christ to every aspect of the system of the old covenant. So what are the implications of this? There are a further 3½ chapters still to come and in these, the writer considers some of the consequences of what he has explained. We will briefly think about some of these implications in the concluding section.

# Conclusion

# Conclusion

## The implications: encouragement and a warning

So what are the implications of the ground-breaking truths that have been revealed in the first 9½ chapters of Hebrews? The writer immediately begins Hebrews 10:19 with a "therefore" and two "sinces" (in verses 19 and 21).

*Because* the work of Christ has resulted in cleansing from sin and moral guilt, and has broken down the barrier between God and man, for the first time since Eden, man can have free access to God. So:

> *Since* we have confidence to enter the Most Holy Place (i.e. heaven itself) by the blood of Jesus... (Hebrews 10:19)

and

> *Since* we have a great priest over the house of God ... (Hebrews 10:21)

Then, a number of things follow on from the wonderful security of the believer's position in Christ. We can approach God with confidence because we have been cleansed of our guilt (verses 22-23); we have the encouragement to hold unswervingly to our hope, because the One who promised is faithful (verse 23); we should therefore encourage one another to love and to serve (verse 24), and keep meeting together for mutual encouragement (verse 25).

The unique claim of the Christian faith is that because of what the Lord Jesus Christ has done for us we can have confidence that we have been forgiven and our guilt has been taken away. We have been made fit for the presence of God because we are in Christ and we have been adopted as His sons and daughters. We therefore do not spend our lives trying by our good behaviour to gain His favour and so be fit to be admitted to His heavenly kingdom. Instead, we can have confidence that we *have* been made fit, by the sacrifice of Christ. He calls us to love and to good works, yes, but that is in response to what He has done for us. He calls us to live up to what we have become through Christ and to live in a manner that is worthy of God's children.

But there are also words of warning from verse 26 onwards. These Jewish believers had all this truth revealed to them – the superiority of Christ to every key feature of Old Testament Judaism – to prophets, to angels, to Moses and Joshua, to the Aaronic priesthood, to the Sinai covenant and the sacrifices belonging to that covenant. Since that is the case, if they reject it, if they go back to Judaism or worse, then what hope is there for them (verses 26-27)? They had just been told that the features of Judaism were intended to be temporary because they were pointing towards the coming Messiah. How could they prefer the imperfect and the ineffective to the perfect and the efficacious? If, having learned all this, they reject Him and turn back they are trampling Him underfoot, despising His blood and insulting the Holy Spirit (verse 29). This will bring fearful punishment (verse 29) and the section ends with the grim warning:

> It is a dreadful thing to fall into the hands of the living God. (Hebrews 10:31)

Many of the Jewish Christians reading this epistle would be scattered throughout the Roman Empire. The temptation for them, especially if they were suffering persecution, may have been to turn away from both their Jewish heritage, and the message of the new covenant, and to follow the pagan practices of the nations in which they lived. The writer calls them to remember the days when they stood firm against opposition in the past (verses 32-34) and to encourage them not to lose their confidence (verses 35-36).

The effectiveness of the work of Christ on the cross, of course, goes far beyond the boundaries of Israel and the Jewish people. His sacrifice opened the way for all men, irrespective of nation or creed, to find a way back to God. As Paul says in 2 Corinthians, God's plan was for the reconciliation, not just of the Jewish people, but of the whole world to Himself.

> Therefore, if anyone is in Christ, he is a new creation; the old has gone, the new has come! All this is from God, who reconciled us to himself, through Christ and gave us the ministry of reconciliation: that God was reconciling the world to himself in Christ, not counting men's sins against them. And he has committed to us the message of reconciliation. (2 Corinthians 5:17-19)

The sacrifice of Christ on the cross, and the way in which this sacrifice cleansed sinful humans of their moral guilt, is explained in Hebrews in the context of God's relationship with Israel. However, this cleansing, and its consequences are foundational to the accomplishment of God's wider purposes also. For example, in Ephesians Paul explains about God's great purpose of reconciliation not just between man and God but between Jew and Gentile, in the creation of the church which is His body. In the past we Gentiles were once

> ... separate from Christ, excluded from citizenship in Israel and foreigners to the covenants of the promise, without

God and without hope in the world. But now in Christ
Jesus you who were once far away have been brought near
by the blood of Christ. For he is our peace, who has made
the two one and destroyed the barrier, the dividing wall of
hostility, by abolishing in his flesh the law with its
commandments and regulations. His purpose was to create
in himself one new man out of the two, thus making peace
and in this one body to reconcile both of them to God
through the cross by which he put to death their
hostility.(Ephesians 2:12-16)

In this tremendous passage we can see echoes of some of the
ideas in Hebrews – the centrality of the blood of Christ to the
whole purpose, the destruction of barriers (in this case between
Jew and Gentile), and the abolition of the Law and all the
regulations that went with it.

Everything has been accomplished through the blood of Christ.
He, the sinless Son of God, humbled Himself to the point of
coming to earth as a man and going to a shameful death on a
cross, a willing victim, so that God's purposes of the
reconciliation of all men to Himself, could be accomplished:

> Therefore God exalted him to the highest place and gave
> him the name that is above every name, that at the name
> of Jesus every knee should bow, in heaven and on earth
> and under the earth, and every tongue confess that Jesus
> Christ is Lord, to the glory of God the Father. (Philippians
> 2:9-11)

He is supreme.

# Bibliography

## Books referred to or quoted in the text

Denney, James, *The Death of Christ,* Tyndale Press

Lewis, C.S. *The Lion, the Witch and the Wardrobe*, Harper
Collins

Penny, Michael, *The New Covenant: Who is it with? When is it
for?* The Open Bible Trust

Stedman, R.C. *Hebrews,* IVP New Testament Commentary Series

Welch, Charles H. and Allen, Stuart *Perfection or Perdition?*
Berean Publishing Trust

Wright, Tom *Hebrews for Everyone,* SPCK

# About the author

W. M. Henry was born in Glasgow in 1949. He qualified as a Chartered Accountant and worked in the accountancy profession for a number of years before moving into academia. At present he is working as an education consultant. He lives in Giffnock with his wife and two daughters. He has recently completed a major work on *The Trinity in John*.

Other publications by W. M. Henry include:

*The Signs in John's Gospel*
*No Condemnation – Romans 5:12-8:39*
*Living in the Truth*
*That you may know – 1 John*
*The Greatness of Christ*
*The Speeches in Acts*
*By Faith Abraham*
*The Making of a Man of God*
*Imitating Christ*

He has also written two books with Michael Penny (which are available both as books and eBooks).

*Following Philippians*
*The Will of God: Past and Present*

Details of all these publications can be seen on
**www.obt.org.uk**

W M Henry is a regular contributor to *Search* magazine

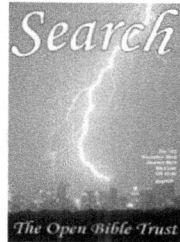

For a free sample of
The Open Bible Trust's magazine *Search*,
please visit

**www.obt.org.uk/search**

or email

**admin@obt.org.uk**

# Further Reading

## The Will of God: Past and Present

**W M Henry and Michael Penny**

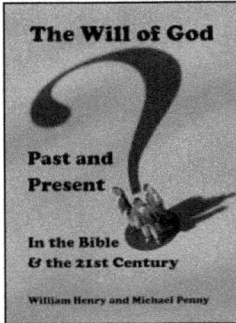

**It is imperative in the study of any subject to consider *all* that the Bible has to say.**

This book does just that: starting in Genesis it works its way through the Bible chronologically.

It pays attention to when new aspects of the will of God are revealed, and to why these changes occur.

In the New Testament, the authors have taken special care to distinguish between the will of God for Jews and His will for Gentiles. Sometimes it is the same ... but not always.

\*\*\*\*\*\*\*\*\*\*\*

Please visit **www.obt.org.uk** for further details of this book and the ones on the next pages.

These books can be ordered from that website.

They are also available as eBooks from Amazon and Apple and as KDP paperbacks from Amazon.

# Following Philippians

## W M Henry & Michael Penny

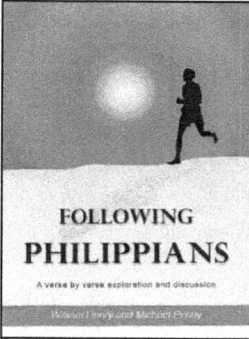

This book from William Henry and Michael Penny is much more than a commentary. It is a verse by verse exploration and discussion.

The authors first examine what a passage would have meant to the original first century Philippians, before seeking applications for 21st century Christians.

Each chapter of the book deals with a particular passage in Philippians in a number of ways.

- First, the Big Issues set out the main points of the passage
- Then the passage is Explored with helpful insights into the historical setting of first century Philippi and the issues of that day
- This is followed by a set of Comprehension Questions on the passage
- Next, the passage is Discussed in a manner which takes what has been learnt and discusses it, using it to direct light onto today's Christian experiences
- Each chapter concludes with a set of Contemplation Questions on the passage.

The result is a study guide to Philippians which balances well-researched historical information with practical lessons for today's Christian.

# Other works by W M Henry include ...

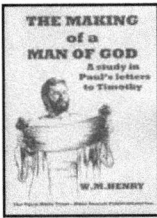

**The Making of a Man of God**
A study in Paul's letters to Timothy

**The Speeches in Acts**

**Living in the truth**
The Message of John's Epistles

**The Signs in John's Gospel**

**Who is Jesus?** (£2.50) Written with Michael Penny

For further details, and a full list, please visit:

## www.obt.org.uk

These books can be ordered from that website.

They are also available as eBooks from Amazon and Apple
and as KDP paperbacks from Amazon

# The Covenants

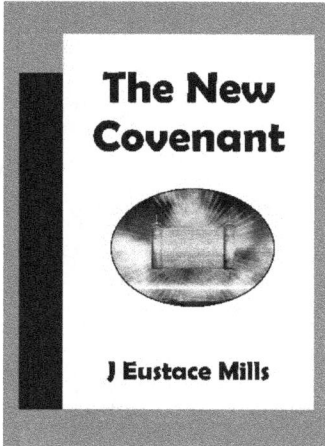

The New Covenant
J Eustace Mills

THE COVENANTS
Ernest Streets

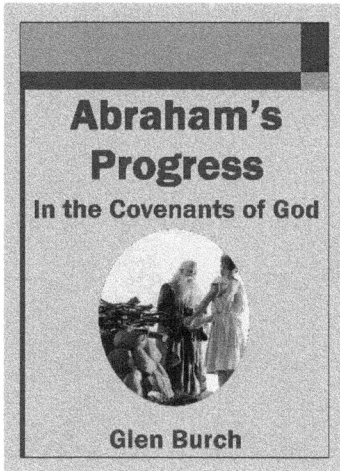

Abraham's Progress
In the Covenants of God
Glen Burch

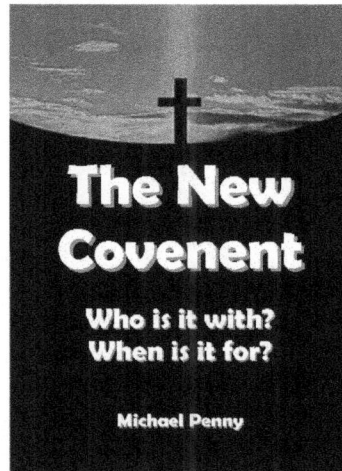

The New Covenent
Who is it with?
When is it for?
Michael Penny

Please visit **www.obt.org.uk** for further details of these books.

These books can be ordered from that website.

They are also available as eBooks from Amazon and Apple
and as KDP paperbacks from Amazon.

*The Superiority of Christ* 99

Publications of The Open Bible Trust must be in accordance with its evangelical, fundamental and dispensational basis. However, beyond this minimum, writers are free to express whatever beliefs they may have as their own understanding, provided that the aim in so doing is to further the objectives of The Open Bible Trust. A copy of the doctrinal basis is available on **www.obt.org.uk** or from:

**THE OPEN BIBLE TRUST**
**Fordland Mount, Upper Basildon,**
**Reading, RG8 8LU, UK**

www.ingramcontent.com/pod-product-compliance
Lightning Source LLC
Chambersburg PA
CBHW070537030426
42337CB00016B/2241